BAREFOOT BOY WITH SHOES ON

Edwin Sánchez

BROADWAY PLAY PUBLISHING INC
New York
www.broadwayplaypublishing.com
info@broadwayplaypublishing.com

BAREFOOT BOY WITH SHOES ON
© 2013 by Edwin Sánchez

All rights reserved. This work is fully protected under the copyright laws of the United States of America. No part of this publication may be photocopied, reproduced, stored in a retrieval system, or transmitted, in any form or by any means, electronic, mechanical, recording, or otherwise, without the prior permission of the publisher. Additional copies of this play are available from the publisher.

Written permission is required for live performance of any sort. This includes readings, cuttings, scenes, and excerpts. For amateur and stock performances, please contact Broadway Play Publishing Inc. For all other rights please contact the author c/o B P P I.

Cover photo by James Leynse
Book design: Marie Donovan
Page make-up: Adobe InDesign
Typeface: Palatino

BAREFOOT BOY WITH SHOES ON premiered at Primary Stages on 20 October 1999. The cast and creative contributors were:

Rosario	Nelson Vasquez
Buelo	Jaime Sanchez
Pops	Lazaro Perez
Morris	Dennis Parlato
Dr Morton	Keith Reddin
Vicky	Abigail López
Director	Casey Childs
Set design	Walt Spangler
Lighting design	Deborah Constantine
Costume design	Debra Stein
Original music/sound design	Fabian Obispo

CHARACTERS & SETTING

Rosario
Buelo
Pops
Morris
Dr Morton
Vicky

The action takes place in the present.

As often as possible, Rosario *should be pulled from one scene to the other.*

(Lights up to a low dim, we see ROSARIO *walking across the stage. He is in pajama bottoms and barefoot. He carries a baby wrapped in a blanket. He sings to his son.)*

ROSARIO: Hey everybody have you heard
I'm gonna buy him a mockingbird
And if that mockingbird don't sing
I'm gonna buy him a—
(Spoken) What baby? What am I gonna buy you? *(He coos to the baby, returns to singing.)*
—diamond ring.
And if that diamond ring don't shine—
(Spoken) Of course it'll shine. I promise you. And your father will never break his promise. *(He continues to walk across the stage.)*

BUELO: *(V O) Dime* Rosario

POPS: *(V O)* Tell me Rosario

DR MORTON: *(V O)* Tell me Rosario

MORRIS: *(V O)* Tell me Rosario

VICKY: *(V O)* Tell me Rosario, where do you go when you want to be alone?

ROSARIO: I close my eyes.

POPS: *(V O)* Rosario!

(Lights out on ROSARIO*)*

POPS: *(V O. Continuing)* Rosario!

(Lights up to reveal a small and cramped room in a S R O [single room occupancy]. There is a bunk bed to one side

where POPS *[*ROSARIO's *father] and* BUELO *[*ROSARIO's *grandfather] sleep.)*

(Also in the room is a small refrigerator with a hot plate on it, a portable T V with a V C R and a small altar off to one side. BUELO *lights a candle and begins to pray. He walks with the use of a cane. Close to the exit of the room is an open fold-away bed where* ROSARIO *is lost under the sheets.* POPS *enters.)*

POPS: You up?

ROSARIO: Not yet.

POPS: You up?

ROSARIO: Not yet.

POPS: You up?

ROSARIO: Dead. Leave the flowers and get out.

POPS: Buelo is waiting for his walk.

(POPS *rips the sheet off* ROSARIO, *who sleeps in his underwear.)*

ROSARIO: For Christ sake, I hardly got any sleep last night.

POPS: That's not Buelo's fault is it?

ROSARIO: *(Under his breath)* Fuck you, Buelo.

POPS: What did you say?! *(Silence)* Your work called, you're starting on the thirteenth floor today. *(He exits.)*

ROSARIO: Nobody has a thirteenth floor.

(BUELO *points to the door.)*

BUELO: *Rosario.*

ROSARIO: Yeah, yeah, keep your shirt on.

(POPS *enters.)*

POPS: Don't forget, you have to see your psychiatrist.

ROSARIO: He's not my psychiatrist.

POPS: Psychiatrist today.

ROSARIO: *(To* BUELO*)* Can't you go for a walk alone, just for today?

POPS: He's afraid.

ROSARIO: There's nothing to be afraid of.

(ROSARIO *dresses for work in full view of* BUELO, *who looks to the floor.)*

ROSARIO: *(Continuing)* He's not a psychiatrist, he's a therapist.

POPS: He's the reason you're not in jail. I already have one son in jail, I don't need another.

(POPS *exits.* BUELO *takes out a pack of cigarettes and shows them to* ROSARIO.*)*

BUELO: *Te compre mas cigarillos.*

ROSARIO: I can get my own cigarettes, thank you very much.

BUELO: *(Shaking his head) No, no puedes.*

(POPS *enters, sits in front of the T V and turns it on.)*

ROSARIO: What are you gonna do today?

POPS: I'm doing it.

ROSARIO: …I saved a little boy.

POPS: When?

ROSARIO: In my dream.

POPS: That doesn't count.

ROSARIO: They lowered me into this tunnel and he grabbed hold of my work boots and then they pulled—

POPS: Your work boots?

ROSARIO: us out. I was very brave. Wasn't scared—

POPS: Your work boots?

ROSARIO: at all, yes Jesus, Mary and Joseph, my fucking work boots.

(POPS *casually smacks the back of* ROSARIO's *head.*)

POPS: You always complaining your boots are too big for you. If he grabbed on to them they probably slid off in his hands.

ROSARIO: No, they didn't.

POPS: And he fell down the tunnel.

ROSARIO: No, he didn't.

POPS: He's probably dead by now.

(BUELO *shrugs and squeezes past* ROSARIO *to sit on the bed and face the TV.*)

ROSARIO: Listen I got some extra money, why don't we all go out to dinner tonight? Someplace nice.

POPS: You ain't gonna cook? There's food here. Cook.

ROSARIO: I won some money.

BUELO: ¿Come fue?

POPS: Where?

ROSARIO: At work. They bet me I wouldn't walk on a ledge with my eyes closed.

POPS: You crazy?! How much you get?

BUELO: ¿Come fue?

ROSARIO: Fifty.

POPS: *Gano cincuenta pesos.*

BUELO: *Mira pa' ya.*

POPS: Let me see.

ROSARIO: You don't have to see. I'm telling you.

POPS: You closed your eyes?

ROSARIO: Yeah. So you want to go out?

POPS: You're crazy. How high were you?

ROSARIO: Twenty six stories.

BUELO: ¿Como fue?

ROSARIO: We can all go to dinner.

POPS: *Vamos a comer afuera.*

BUELO: *Esta bueno.*

(ROSARIO *is finished dressing.* POPS *helps* BUELO *stand and hands him his cane.*)

POPS: Chinese, right?

ROSARIO: No, I was thinking some place nice.

POPS: You don't want to spend all your money on one meal.

ROSARIO: Yes I do.

POPS: That's stupid.

ROSARIO: We can have something nice! What, the nice police is gonna take it away from us?

BUELO: ¿Como fue?

ROSARIO: We should all, you know, dress up a little.

POPS: I'm going like this. I'm comfortable.

BUELO: ¿Comida china, verdad?

ROSARIO: No, not Chinese food. Something different tonight. Fancy food.

POPS: You know your grandfather's digestion. He can't eat just anything.

ROSARIO: They have bland food.

POPS: How do you know?

BUELO: ¿Como fue?

POPS: You go to restaurants all the time?

ROSARIO: They got menus, you know, and we can just pick something.

BUELO: *¿Por que no lo va y lo busca y lo trae de vuelta?*

ROSARIO: What?

POPS: Yeah, why don't you go get it and bring it back on your way home?

ROSARIO: Cause the point is to go out.

BUELO: *Que no se olvide los dumplings.*

POPS: Yeah, don't—

ROSARIO: We're not doing Chinese!

POPS: —forget the dumplings. Boiled.

(ROSARIO *turns off the T V.*)

ROSARIO: I got a little extra money. Let's go out, the three of us, cause we never do.

POPS: You go ahead. *(He turns it on.)*

ROSARIO: No. No with the T V. *(He squeezes in to turn off the T V.)*

POPS: I'm gonna be tired tonight.

ROSARIO: Of what? You never do anything.

(BUELO *turns it on again.*)

BUELO: *Que traiga cerveza.*

(ROSARIO *turns off the T V.*)

ROSARIO: *No, no cerveza.*

(POPS *turns on the T V.*)

ROSARIO: Wine. Tonight we have wine.

POPS: I never do anything?! I never do anything?!

ROSARIO: Okay, okay, you do stuff.

POPS: If you live to be a hundred you'll never work as hard as I did for you and your mother. And for what?

ROSARIO: Okay, okay.

POPS: For her to die on me. Don't forget, mister, you're taking care of me now cause I took care of you. For years.

BUELO: *¿Como fue?*

ROSARIO: Okay, okay. I'll bring back some take out when I come home. Everybody okay with Chinese, right? *(Silence)* And beer? How about some ice cream? *(He touches* POPS' *shoulder.)* I'm sorry.

(POPS *nods without looking at him.* ROSARIO *helps* BUELO *stand. They move to the door.)*

ROSARIO: Hey, maybe I can bring back another porno film.

BUELO: *¿Como fue?*

POPS: Triple X.

BUELO: *Hombre si.*

(ROSARIO *takes a necktie off a hook and goes to a small area where he faces out to the audience. He is in the bathroom. He carefully makes the knot in his tie. When he is done, he decides he's not happy with it and starts over again. He has left* BUELO *in the hallway waiting for him.* BUELO *bangs his cane on the floor, outside of the bathroom, hurrying* ROSARIO *along.)*

BUELO: *(Continuing) Cuatro, doce, diezinueve, vientiuno*

ROSARIO: How much money do you think you've spent on playing the numbers, huh? More than you'll probably ever win.

BUELO: *Cuatro, doce—*

ROSARIO: Hey I got it! I heard you. Spend a thousand years here and never learn English. You know what that is? That is willful ignorance.

(ROSARIO *exits the bathroom.* BUELO *timidly offers him a cigarette. They start off for* BUELO's *daily walk, with* BUELO *leaning heavily on both his cane and* ROSARIO.)

BUELO: *Cada persona nace con su suerte. Yo tengo mi suerte.*

ROSARIO: Yeah, *suerte. Mala, muy mala.* Very bad luck. (*He smokes.*) If I weren't here, if I ran away, who would walk you? Hey, Buelo, you a dog you gotta be walked? *¿Habla usted el arf arf?*

(BUELO *smiles, not understanding, he pats* ROSARIO's *arm.*)

BUELO: Good boy.

(BUELO *stops and looks up to a tall building. It is a male correctional facility where* ROSARIO's *brother is.* BUELO *waves and, in the same manner* POPS *did, nonchalantly hits* ROSARIO *on the back of the head.* ROSARIO *smiles a fake smile, and waves to his brother. He salutes him with his cigarette, taking a long puff.*)

ROSARIO: Only ninety nine more years and he'll be back home with his loving family where he belongs.

BUELO: *Mala suerte. Maldita suerte.*

ROSARIO: Yeah, imagine that prison guard landing on Junior's knife that way. Junior's your favorite, isn't he?

(BUELO *kisses* ROSARIO.)

BUELO: *Tu eres bueno.*

(ROSARIO *is taken aback. He helps* BUELO *on his walk back.*)

ROSARIO: You know if Pops finds out we stand outside of Junior's jail everyday he'll be real angry. Junior is dead to him. I'm the only one he loves now. How about that? Junior was supposed to accomplish everything and he winds up in prison.

BUELO: *Maldita suerte.*

ROSARIO: Everybody's born with their luck. Can I have another cigarette? *(He mimes smoking.)*

BUELO: No.

ROSARIO: Please.

BUELO: *Mala suerte.*

ROSARIO: Hey, you wanna do an experiment?

(ROSARIO *takes* BUELO's *cane in his hands, he slices the air with it, relishing the sound it makes.*)

BUELO: *¿Como fue?*

(ROSARIO *closes* BUELO's *eyes and slices the air very close to him with the cane.* BUELO *opens his eyes in fear.*)

ROSARIO: No, you're not supposed to open your eyes.

(ROSARIO *closes* BUELO's *eyes again, who opens them again,* ROSARIO *again closes them and again* BUELO *opens them.* ROSARIO *slaps* BUELO's *face.*)

ROSARIO: *(Continuing)* No, keep them closed.

(BUELO *opens them again.* ROSARIO *slaps him again. They are not hard slaps, but they are humiliating.* BUELO *begins to cry.*)

ROSARIO: *(Continuing)* No, don't cry.

BUELO: *Por favor.*

(ROSARIO *closes* BUELO's *eyes again.*)

ROSARIO: This is an experiment.

(BUELO *gives him two more cigarettes,* ROSARIO *pushes them away.*)

ROSARIO: *(Continuing)* Don't you trust me, Buelo?

(BUELO *puts the cigarettes away and closes his eyes.* ROSARIO *brings the cane up over* BUELO's *head only instead of moving it he imitates the sound it makes.*)

ROSARIO: Whoosh!

(BUELO's *hands fly up to his face in fear, but he doesn't dare open his eyes.* ROSARIO *removes his hands and opens his eyes.*)

ROSARIO: Good Buelo. (*He puts the cane back in* BUELO's *hand.*) Whoosh. That's the sound that fear makes. Come on, let's play your numbers.

(*Through the course of the scene they have walked to the S R O where* ROSARIO *leaves* BUELO *and walks directly into his scene with* DR MORTON.)

(DR MORTON *speaks to* ROSARIO *as if he were in his office.*)

DR MORTON: Rosario, sit down.

(ROSARIO *remains where he is.*)

DR MORTON: I'm going to have to start writing a report on you if you don't sit down.

(ROSARIO *goes to* DR MORTON's *office and sits.* VICKY *is there.*)

VICKY: I knew he would sit.

DR MORTON: *(To* VICKY) Please.

VICKY: He's so predictable.

(DR MORTON *holds his hand up.*)

DR MORTON: We are not making any progress here.

VICKY: That's cause the only progress he'll accept is me saying that it's his baby, and it's not.

ROSARIO: We were together for two years.

VICKY: Don't remind me.

ROSARIO: I know you didn't cheat on me.

VICKY: What? You got a ouija board?

ROSARIO: He's gonna look just like me. My grandfather has baby pictures of me and I guarantee you, I bet you anything, he's gonna look just like me.

VICKY: No, he's gonna look like his father.

ROSARIO: And that's me.

VICKY: In your dreams.

DR MORTON: We can always do a blood test.

(Silence. ROSARIO and VICKY stare at each other.)

VICKY: …Okay.

ROSARIO: No.

VICKY: Let's do it.

ROSARIO: I am not taking no test! *(He slams his fist on the table. Silence.)*

VICKY: At least this time it wasn't my face. I'm glad you're seeing him as he really is, Doctor.

ROSARIO: Women. *(Small laugh)* My father always [warned me.]

VICKY: Your father spends all day watching porno. Sometimes the same tape over and over. And you come home from work and just sit down right next to him.

ROSARIO: I don't do [that.]

VICKY: Oh no, not much.

DR MORTON: I don't think we need to bring up [the past.]

VICKY: No, I'm tired. I am tired of having to be careful cause his fists don't have warning lights. Okay, I dropped the complaint, but that was on the condition that he got counseling.

ROSARIO: Which I'm doing.

VICKY: You lie during the counseling sessions. How is that helping?

ROSARIO: I don't lie. …I stopped hitting you.

VICKY: No, you stopped hitting the thing that was carrying "your" baby.

ROSARIO: See? It's mine.

VICKY: The second I pop that kid you're gonna be smacking me all over again. Shit.

(ROSARIO *tries to comfort* VICKY.)

VICKY: Don't. Rosario, this is so not your baby that if I have to dig up the rustiest wire hanger and rip it out of me I will.

(ROSARIO *leaps over the desk and goes for* VICKY's *throat.* DR MORTON *blocks him.*)

DR MORTON: Sit. Sit down! Both of you.

ROSARIO: I want to swear out a complaint.

DR MORTON: Rosario please.

ROSARIO: I want to swear out a complaint for attempted murder. If you try to kill my baby—

VICKY: You'll what?

(ROSARIO *stares at* VICKY *and nods his head.*)

ROSARIO: Okay, okay.

DR MORTON: Okay what?

(ROSARIO *crosses himself and begins to pray.*)

VICKY: Oh, this is new, he never prays. This is for your benefit, Doctor. Enjoy it. Look, even if the baby is his it is not his. You got that? You're the professional here. You make him understand.

(*She exits.* ROSARIO *rises to follow her.*)

DR MORTON: Rosario, be a good boy. Don't.

(ROSARIO *stares at the door where* VICKY *just exited.*)

ROSARIO: Okay. I can be a good boy. I can be a good boy.

DR MORTON: You still call her and hang up, don't you.

ROSARIO: I never…yes, sir.

DR MORTON: I think it's safe to say she doesn't want to see you again.

ROSARIO: You don't know her like I do. I was her first.

DR MORTON: Rosario.

ROSARIO: Fine. Just let her give me my baby.

DR MORTON: You never married her. Legally it's her baby.

ROSARIO: Yeah, we'll see. You know, I don't have to come here.

DR MORTON: Oh?

ROSARIO: She tried to press charges but she couldn't.

DR MORTON: That's because your grandfather backed up your story that she fell down the stairs.

ROSARIO: Cause that's what happened.

DR MORTON: You still take no responsibility for your actions, do you?

ROSARIO: You don't think we're gonna get back together again? Fine. You're the one who's gonna look like a fool.

DR MORTON: Do you think I'm against you?

ROSARIO: Can I go now?

DR MORTON: You didn't answer my question.

ROSARIO: No, of course not. I am loved and respected by all.

(DR MORTON *hands* ROSARIO *a paper cup.*)

DR MORTON: Could you please step into the men's room and give me a urine sample?

(ROSARIO *stares at* DR MORTON.)

DR MORTON: It's a simple random drug test.

ROSARIO: I don't feel like peeing.

DR MORTON: Luckily I'm sure we both have nothing better to do than wait.

(ROSARIO *takes the paper cup and exits.*)

DR MORTON: This is also a precaution for you. You're a window washer, what if you had some, let's say, recreational drug. You might fall and kill yourself, worse, you might fall on someone and kill them. We have to think of those things. It's obvious that you don't. You seem to believe the world's problems begin and end with you. You are not the center of the universe.

(ROSARIO *enters with the cup.*)

ROSARIO: What did you say?

DR MORTON: I said you have a lot to learn.

(ROSARIO *shows* DR MORTON *the cup.*)

ROSARIO: Is this enough?

DR MORTON: More than enough.

ROSARIO: You sure?

DR MORTON: Very.

ROSARIO: In that case. (*He drinks a swig of his own urine.*) As long as it's more than enough.

(DR MORTON *and* ROSARIO *stare at each other.* DR MORTON *swallows, taps his clip board.* ROSARIO *is about to leave.*)

DR MORTON: No, sit down.

ROSARIO: My hour's up.

DR MORTON: I'm feeling generous today.

ROSARIO: I can't be late for [work.]

DR MORTON: Sit. I'll call them.

(ROSARIO *sits*.)

DR MORTON: Perhaps you'd like another sip. *(Silence)* Rosario, for future reference, I don't shock easily and there's nothing I hate more than grandstanding. Are we clear on that? Good. Now, your employers seem to be happy with your work habits. No complaints. You have no fear about working on the taller buildings?

ROSARIO: The higher the better. *(He goes to window sill and sets himself up as if he were outside a window he were washing. He continues to talk to* DR MORTON.*)* It's a great job. I look in on all these beautiful places and no one ever sees me. I'm like a fly on the wall. I'm invisible. I've seen people fight, make love and it's like I was never there. *(He secures himself to the window with the hooks on either side of his belt. He begins to wash the window. He looks inside the room and studies it, his fingertips on the glass.)* Someday. This will all be my son's. All this. And everything else. Rich people are different, it's not just that they own everything. They're different.

DR MORTON: How?

(Chopin's Fantasie Impromptu *is heard.)*

ROSARIO: *(Speaking into the apartment)* Hello?

(The music follows ROSARIO *into the bathroom where he very ceremoniously makes his tie as he imagines a rich person would.)*

POPS: Rosario! Hey, Rosario.

(ROSARIO *makes his knot tighter, trying to choke himself. He flushes and opens the door. Music out)*

ROSARIO: Okay.

POPS: You shit cakes? I never smell anything when you go to the bathroom.

ROSARIO: Do we have to discuss this?

(ROSARIO *walks to the room and sits on the bed.* BUELO *is watching T V.*)

ROSARIO: You don't even understand it, why are you watching it?

POPS: What's to understand? It's a porno tape.

BUELO: Triple X.

(POPS *snaps his fingers.*)

POPS: Beer.

(ROSARIO *reaches for three beers in the refrigerator. Hands one to each of them and keeps one for himself. He sits on the bed, facing away from the T V.*)

ROSARIO: She's coming back.

(*Sounds of porno tape*)

POPS: Who?

ROSARIO: The mother of my baby. She told me.

POPS: Vicky said she'd never set foot in this place [again.]

ROSARIO: She changed her mind! You never changed your mind? She is coming back, but we can't be watching porno no more. That makes her angry.

(POPS *opens his beer can.*)

ROSARIO: And no more beer.

(BUELO *opens his beer can.*)

ROSARIO: Cause she's a lady, you know. (*He sips.*) And ladies don't like that.

(POPS *and* BUELO *sit, transfixed by the images on the screen.*)

POPS: If I were a young man, I would be a dog. I'd have women hanging all over me.

ROSARIO: She's coming back soon and I don't want *(He sees the screen.)* and I don't want… *(He sits on the floor, in front of the screen.)* Isn't she pretty?

(ROSARIO starts calling out VICKY's name from the S R O. He continues as he reaches her door and begins banging on it. He is a little drunk.)

ROSARIO: *(Continuing)* Vicky! Vicky! Hey, Vicky, Rosario's here. It's himself, in the flesh.

VICKY: *(O S)* Shut up.

ROSARIO: Look who's back. Special return engagement.

VICKY: *(O S)* Shut the hell up.

(VICKY opens the door a crack. ROSARIO and VICKY stare at each other.)

ROSARIO: First stop on my world tour.

(He tries to open the door, she stands in the doorway.)

ROSARIO: *(Continuing)* Missed you today. Missed you yesterday, too.

(ROSARIO runs his hand gently across VICKY's face.)

VICKY: Too bad you didn't miss me last time.

(ROSARIO stops.)

ROSARIO: See, and I'm trying to be real nice here.

VICKY: That's just the trouble, you gotta try.

(ROSARIO tries to go past VICKY.)

VICKY: You're not coming in.

ROSARIO: I don't think that's the question.

VICKY: No, but that's the answer.

COP: *(O S)* Vicky…

VICKY: *(Answering COP)* It's just my cousin.

COP: *(O S)* Are you sure?

VICKY: Am I sure I know who my cousin is?!

ROSARIO: And who's he? Who's that sleeping in my bed?

VICKY: That has never been your bed.

(ROSARIO *roughly grabs her belly.*)

ROSARIO: This tells me it's my bed.

COP: *(O S)* Vicky.

ROSARIO: Answer him.

VICKY: Yeah?

COP: *(O S)* Bring me something sweet when you come back.

(ROSARIO *tries to push* VICKY *aside. She grabs the doorframe and won't budge.*)

ROSARIO: Let go of the door.

VICKY: No.

ROSARIO: Let go of the door.

VICKY: No.

ROSARIO: Last time, I said let go of the door. *(He is about to hit her.)*

VICKY: He's a cop, Rosario.

(ROSARIO *stops.*)

VICKY: Hit me now.

ROSARIO: He ain't no fucking [cop]

VICKY: Badge 37314. Officer J Clark. Hit me now. *(Pause)* You forget how?

(VICKY *takes* ROSARIO*'s hand, balls it up and puts it against her face. He pulls his hand away.*)

ROSARIO: I hit you once.

VICKY: Twice, three times. Isn't that funny, I lost count, too.

ROSARIO: …You got me mad.

VICKY: And I apologized. Every time.

ROSARIO: Get him out.

VICKY: We sleep with his revolver right next to us. Officer J Clark has even taught me how to fire it. I'm good, Rosario. Either one of us could take you out.

(ROSARIO *tries to touch* VICKY's *belly, but can't bring himself to do it.*)

ROSARIO: That's my baby.

VICKY: No, it's my baby. After the last time you hit me I knew what I had to do. If I'm gonna be a woman I'm gonna have to stop playing with little boys. Like you, Rosario. *(She cups her hand over his penis.)* I went from a boy to a man.

COP: *(O S)* Hey, Vicky.

VICKY: *(In his ear, seductively)* Hit me now.

(ROSARIO *takes a step back.*)

ROSARIO: If I hurt you, I'm sorry.

VICKY: If?

COP: *(O S)* Don't forget, something sweet.

(VICKY *is closing the door.*)

VICKY: I thought I would enjoy this more.

ROSARIO: It ain't over. *(He exits.)*

VICKY: It ain't nothing but over. *(She closes the door.)*

(ROSARIO *secures himself to the window with the hooks on either side of his belt. He begins to wash the window, soaping it first, then using a squeegee to get rid of most of the water.*)

(Chopin's Fantasie Impromptu *is heard.* MORRIS *enters the room. He begins to massage his neck and then begins to fondle himself.* ROSARIO *taps on the glass.)*

ROSARIO: Excuse me, I can see you.

(MORRIS *ignores him and begins to undress while continuing to play with himself.)*

ROSARIO: *(Continuing)* Mister! Excuse me. Live person behind you. Hey! I can see you.

(MORRIS *turns to face* ROSARIO.)

MORRIS: Well, that's kind of the point. Do come in.

ROSARIO: Uh, no thank you.

MORRIS: I don't bite.

ROSARIO: What do you want with me?

(MORRIS *walks to the window, opens it.)*

ROSARIO: Careful.

MORRIS: Please don't tell me about safety. Come in.

ROSARIO: Why?

(MORRIS *goes for* ROSARIO, *forcing him to lean as far back as he can.)*

ROSARIO: Hey, watch it.

MORRIS: Come in.

ROSARIO: I gotta go.

MORRIS: One hundred dollars says you gotta stay.

ROSARIO: I don't do that.

MORRIS: Do what? Earn money? One hundred dollars.

ROSARIO: I don't think so.

(MORRIS *reaches out and unhooks one of* ROSARIO's *safety straps.)*

ROSARIO: Are you fucking crazy!

MORRIS: I always get what I want.

ROSARIO: I'll rip your fucking heart out!

MORRIS: You'd have to come inside to do that.

(ROSARIO *hesitates, unhooks his other safety strap, jumps inside. He punches* MORRIS, *who puts his hands up to protect his face.*)

MORRIS: *(Continuing)* Not the face. You can hit me anywhere else, but not the face.

ROSARIO: You could have killed me.

MORRIS: That's right, I could have. I've been watching you for a long time.

ROSARIO: No one ever sees me.

MORRIS: I know your schedule by heart. And I've contented myself with just looking, but today…

ROSARIO: What about today?

MORRIS: Martini? *(He makes himself a drink. Continuing)* I saw a boy I had kept, on and off for about a year. I had lost track of him. I saw him today and he was sick. Very sick.

ROSARIO: Did you give it to him?

MORRIS: Certainly not. I was lucky he didn't give it to me. He saw me on the street, I was being questioned by a reporter on…something. And the boy pushed his way to the front of the crowd and just stared at me. He is ashamed to be sick, as well he should be, and he wanted me to be ashamed too.

ROSARIO: Did you say anything to him?

MORRIS: You're very good looking but you're very stupid. Of course not. He is a political liability. As are you, I dare say.

ROSARIO: I don't vote.

MORRIS: Will wonders never cease.

ROSARIO: Don't condescend to me cause I got too much ammunition.

MORRIS: Right you are. You're a nice straight man, aren't you?

ROSARIO: Yeah.

MORRIS: One hundred dollars, every time we meet. And you have to promise not to let any other man touch you.

ROSARIO: No.

MORRIS: Two hundred. And before we get into a bidding frenzy that's exactly what the market will bear, two hundred. Tops.

ROSARIO: No.

MORRIS: Three hundred.

ROSARIO: I thought you said two hundred was tops.

MORRIS: I lied. I'm in politics. It's expected.

ROSARIO: I can't.

MORRIS: You don't have to do anything.

ROSARIO: I can't. I'm gonna be a father soon. I don't want my son to be ashamed of me.

(MORRIS *is about to offer* ROSARIO *a drink, refreshes his own instead.*)

MORRIS: Take off your shirt.

ROSARIO: No. It's all sweaty. (*He heads for the window.*)

MORRIS: I'll take mine off. In fact, let's trade. Mine's custom made.

ROSARIO: Mine has my name on it.

MORRIS: Rosario.

(MORRIS' *fingers barely touch the name on* ROSARIO's *shirt.* MORRIS *reaches into his wallet and puts a hundred dollar bill into his own shirt pocket, he then holds up the shirt to* ROSARIO.)

MORRIS: Trade you. I know a lot of important people.

(ROSARIO *hesitates.*)

ROSARIO: Who do you know who's important?

MORRIS: Everybody. My clients are politicians for the most part. Senators, congressmen, a couple of governors.

(ROSARIO *begins to unbutton his shirt.*)

ROSARIO: And they come to you?

MORRIS: Indeed they do. I help them get elected. I get invited to their homes. I meet celebrities.

ROSARIO: You ever meet Madonna?

MORRIS: Not yet, but I'm sure it's just a matter of time.

(ROSARIO *pulls his shirt out of his pants.*)

ROSARIO: Famous people are different, right?

MORRIS: Different how?

ROSARIO: You know, everybody knows who they are.

MORRIS: Yes, dear.

(MORRIS *stares at* ROSARIO. *He holds out his shirt to him.* ROSARIO *takes his off.*)

ROSARIO: Hold it a second. (*He checks through his shirt pockets to make sure they are empty.*) Okay. Just wanted to make sure I didn't have anything in my pockets.

(ROSARIO *extends his shirt and he and* MORRIS *exchange shirts.*)

ROSARIO: You ever get anybody famous you don't like?

MORRIS: If they can pay me I like them.

(MORRIS *puts on* ROSARIO's *shirt while* ROSARIO *just holds his.*)

ROSARIO: What if it's a politician you don't agree with?

MORRIS: I agree with all the checks that clear.

ROSARIO: Yeah, but what if like, in your case, you're gay, and they're anti—

MORRIS: *(Cutting him off)* In the first place my life is none of their concern

ROSARIO: Okay.

MORRIS: and in the second place I am a business man. I would help elect the devil himself if he paid me enough. You know, the only smart thing you've said since you came in here was "I don't vote".

(ROSARIO *throws* MORRIS's *shirt on the floor and heads for the window.*)

MORRIS: Oh, don't be stupid, at least take the money.

(ROSARIO *picks up the shirt.*)

MORRIS: Rosario…you're a bright man. If I wouldn't help them get elected someone else would. And why should someone else get the money? You know *(He puts his arm around* ROSARIO's *shoulders.)* whenever I have to go to some "anti" gay rally, I just smile. Yes I do. Inside I'm laughing at them. Because I snuck in. Into the rally, into their lives. They can't see me and I'm right there. Could I change their minds if I said I was…not like them? No, they'd still hate. They'd just have one more person to hate, that's all. This way at least I get their money. That's what you have to do with the enemy; let them think you're one of them. You can understand that, can't you?

(ROSARIO *takes* MORRIS's *hand off his shoulder.*)

ROSARIO: Tell me, does it work the same way for a black surrounded by racists? Should he just pretend he's white? You're a bright man, get back to me.

(ROSARIO *heads to the window, followed by* MORRIS.)

MORRIS: Well, a brain is an unexpected bonus. You'll come back, won't you? *(Pause)* Don't make me say the "P" word.

ROSARIO: I gotta—

MORRIS: Please

ROSARIO: —go.

MORRIS: Well, when you gotta go you gotta go. *(Pause)* Rosario.

ROSARIO: Yeah?

MORRIS: He amused me, like I think you will. He used to be so beautiful. That's what's missing in your life, beauty.

ROSARIO: How do you know what's missing in my life?

MORRIS: That's why you're so angry. There are two things a true survivor can smell, anger and fear. I am a survivor. And so are you.

(ROSARIO *climbs out the window.*)

MORRIS: Come back when you want to tell me why you're so angry. *(Yelling after* ROSARIO. *Continuing)* I'll give you two hundred dollars for your pants!

(ROSARIO *is buttoning his new shirt. He stands in front of the mirror of his room in the S R O. He puts on a tie. Enter* POPS.)

POPS: What's with the shirt?

ROSARIO: They lost mine at work so they gave me this one.

POPS: It's a good shirt.

ROSARIO: Yeah, well it was just lying around.

(POPS *tries to touch the shirt,* ROSARIO *moves away, still tying his tie.*)

ROSARIO: Your fly's open.

(POPS *ignores him.*)

POPS: You shouldn't wear one of those three for five dollar ties with that shirt. That's a quality shirt.

ROSARIO: How would you know? (*He exits.*)

POPS: I know.

(*Lights up on* VICKY. ROSARIO *stops her on the street.*)

ROSARIO: Can we just talk—

VICKY: No, and get out of my way.

(ROSARIO *gently reaches for* VICKY, *she pushes his hand away.*)

ROSARIO: —a little?

VICKY: I got his gun in my bag.

ROSARIO: I could just take his gun and smack you over the head with it. (*Silence*) I'm sorry. (*Silence*) I got a gift for my baby.

VICKY: The baby don't want nothing from you.

ROSARIO: Doesn't want anything.

VICKY: Excuse me, are you correcting my English, mother fucker?

ROSARIO: Please take the present.

VICKY: No.

ROSARIO: Please.

VICKY: No.

(ROSARIO *holds out a blue Tiffany box.*)

ROSARIO: Open it.

(VICKY *doesn't.*)

VICKY: All I want is to get past you.

(ROSARIO *opens the box. Inside is a silver spoon.*)

ROSARIO: It's for my baby.

(VICKY *studies* ROSARIO.)

VICKY: How much did that cost?

ROSARIO: It cost…it cost a lot.

VICKY: How much did that cost you? A hundred? Two hundred?

ROSARIO: He can tell people he was born with a silver spoon in his mouth. That's how important people are born.

VICKY: What difference is that spoon gonna make?

(VICKY *knocks it out of* ROSARIO's *hand.*)

ROSARIO: Pick it up.

VICKY: And for what? So people will think he's something he's not?

ROSARIO: Pick it up! (*He pulls her bag off her shoulder and throws it on the ground. Silence*) Pick up the spoon.

(VICKY *tries to move her bag with her foot,* ROSARIO *pushes her. Pause. She picks up the spoon.*)

ROSARIO: Now say "thank you".

(*Silence*)

VICKY: (*Softly*) Thank you. (*Louder*) Thank you.

(*Silence*)

ROSARIO: You're welcome. (*He throws her purse at her.*) Cops die, you know. And all of a sudden you wind up alone. All alone.

(ROSARIO *steps aside and bows, indicating that* VICKY *should pass. She warily does. She goes directly to* DR MORTON's *office.*)

VICKY: He's never gonna leave me alone. He thinks I belong to him, like property, you know. So that means the baby belongs to him, too. No, no way, I'm sorry. He's gonna squeeze a crib into that room the Cortez men share, or worse yet, Rosario will sleep with the baby. Father and mother all rolled up in one. If he could he would beat the milk out of me so he could be the one breast feeding the kid.

DR MORTON: Do you need a second to pull yourself together?

VICKY: No, no I'm okay.

(ROSARIO *goes to* DR MORTON's *office. He overhears from outside the conversation between* VICKY *and* DR MORTON.)

DR MORTON: You have a right to think of yourself and your future, Vicky. And the baby's future. You've made a very wise decision.

VICKY: Please don't. I made a decision, period. I'm gonna sell the baby to your friends, they'll give me enough money and I can start my life over again.

(ROSARIO *takes a step back as if he had been punched. He hits himself in the stomach, over and over again.*)

VICKY: And you just tell Rosario…you tell him anything. Tell him I died.

DR MORTON: I'll take care of Rosario. They're good people, they'll give your son a fine home.

VICKY: Are they white people?

DR MORTON: I never think of them that way.

VICKY: Hey, I'm asking, that's all. Like I got no right to know?

DR MORTON: I don't think of them that way.

VICKY: All right, that means they are.

(ROSARIO *enters, pretending not to have heard anything.*)

DR MORTON: You're early.

ROSARIO: I'm trying to better myself, doctor.

DR MORTON: That's…commendable.

(ROSARIO *sits by* VICKY. *He takes her hand in a very gentle and loving way. He looks at her.*)

VICKY: What? What?!

DR MORTON: Rosario.

ROSARIO: Gimme back my ring.

(VICKY *pulls her hand away. She and* DR MORTON *stare at* ROSARIO.)

ROSARIO: The one I gave you.

VICKY: I know which one. *(Silence. She takes it off and stares at it.)* This reminded me that it wasn't all bad. That we had some nice times, too. That's the only reason I wanted to keep it.

ROSARIO: Yeah, well, I have someone else I want to give it to.

(VICKY *puts the ring in* ROSARIO's *palm, she is staring daggers into him.*)

VICKY: I hope you make her just as happy as you made me.

ROSARIO: Thank you.

DR MORTON: So, you have someone else. I take it then it really is over between you two.

ROSARIO: Uh huh. I gotta go.

VICKY: We didn't talk about the baby.

ROSARIO: No, we didn't. *(He exits.)*

VICKY: …I'm supposed to feel better. Why don't I?

(BUELO *comes up to* ROSARIO *as he exits* DR MORTON's *office. They walk together.*)

BUELO: *Cuatro, doce, diezinueve, veintiuno. Algun dia tengo que ganar.*

(BUELO *hands a cigarette to* ROSARIO *who lights it. He speaks in very bad English.*)

BUELO: Someday I win!

ROSARIO: Vicky's going away, Buelo. And she's never coming back. You gonna miss her?

BUELO: *¿Como fue?*

ROSARIO: Sure you will.

(*Chopin's* Grande Polonaise Brillante Op 22 *begins to play.* ROSARIO *appears at* MORRIS's *window.*)

MORRIS: As things weigh you down you must dispose of them. Look at you, look at what you do.

ROSARIO: I wash windows.

MORRIS: Is that what you want your son to do?

(ROSARIO *enters* MORRIS's *area.*)

ROSARIO: No.

(MORRIS *conducts an imaginary orchestra.*)

MORRIS: Sublime. …What do you want for your son?

ROSARIO: A crib.

MORRIS: That's it? You flaming idiot.

(ROSARIO *pushes* MORRIS.)

MORRIS: Flaming fool?

(ROSARIO *pushes* MORRIS *again.*)

MORRIS: Flaming…

ROSARIO: You get one more try, old man before you need bridge work.

MORRIS: Flaming…you. I'm sorry. Fool seems to be the kindest one I can think of. Martini? I was just about to have one. You can't strike a man offering you alcohol. It's a rule.

ROSARIO: Says who?

MORRIS: Says me. I'm a rich, old, white man. I get to make the rules. I see you have another "Rosario" shirt.

ROSARIO: It's my uniform.

MORRIS: Ah yes, I've always been so drawn to our boys in uniform.

ROSARIO: I'm not a boy.

MORRIS: Little joke. *(Hands him a drink)* Cheers.

ROSARIO: No toast?

MORRIS: That was just it, dear.

(ROSARIO *walks around.*)

ROSARIO: You got nice stuff. I mean, you can tell it's tasteful. My son's gonna have taste.

MORRIS: Well, lucky for him he'll have you as a role model.

ROSARIO: Yeah. You didn't just insult me, did you?

(MORRIS *takes a sip,* ROSARIO *takes* MORRIS's *drink and downs it.*)

MORRIS: Easy now, big fella. You're going to be thirty seven stories above the street.

ROSARIO: What did you have to do to get all this?

MORRIS: Watch my manners, eat all my vegetables.

ROSARIO: No, really, tell me. You born rich?

MORRIS: Hardly.

ROSARIO: So what's the secret?

MORRIS: I forget.

(Pause. ROSARIO hands MORRIS back the glass.)

ROSARIO: No, you don't. You just don't want to tell me. It's okay. My son will find out.

MORRIS: I pity you if he does. *(Pause)* Thirty seven stories up. The higher you go the more you must depend on your balance, on keeping your focus. You don't get up to the top and start admiring the view. When you get to the top, the first thing you do, the very first is to say, "Bullshit, this is not the top", and look for something higher. Don't carry anything that can hold you back. Get rid of it. Now in your case you're a lovely mediocre person so why should you change? I'll give you five hundred dollars for your pants.

ROSARIO: No…yes.

MORRIS: Too late.

(ROSARIO starts unbuckling his pants.)

ROSARIO: Wait a second.

MORRIS: It was a one time offer.

ROSARIO: It took me by surprise.

MORRIS: I'm not interested anymore.

ROSARIO: Four hundred…and I'll take them off right now.

MORRIS: Oh, look at the time.

ROSARIO: Three hundred. *(He has pulled them half off.)* Man, this is a quality pair of pants.

MORRIS: Seventy five.

ROSARIO: Are you nuts!? You gave me one hundred for the shirt.

MORRIS: Fifty.

ROSARIO: What happened to seventy five?

MORRIS: Thanks for coming by. Oh. *(Looks at window)* I think you left a spot on my window. Please take care of it before you leave.

(MORRIS turns his back on ROSARIO, who reluctantly pulls up his pants and is about to climb out the window.)

MORRIS: You could have had the five hundred, but you hesitated. Kinda the story of your life, isn't it?

(ROSARIO is about to hit MORRIS who doesn't even turn around.)

MORRIS: If that's the only way you know how to play, the game is, as of now, officially over.

(ROSARIO returns to the window.)

MORRIS: I'm sure you can scrape together enough money for a passable crib, if not the government will surely provide you with one. Your kind gets all the breaks.

(VICKY is outside ROSARIO's S R O. She is wearing dark glasses and carrying a bag of groceries. She walks up to the door, hesitates, turns away and turns again to the door. She hears someone approaching and turns to see BUELO, with great difficulty walking towards the S R O.)

VICKY: Here, let me help you. Did Rosario leave you alone?

BUELO: *Cuatro, doce, diezinueve, veintiuno.*

VICKY: He went to play your numbers, huh.

(VICKY helps him sit. She sits next to him and smoothes his hair.)

VICKY: *(Continuing)* Did Rosario take you to get a haircut? You look so nice.

(BUELO looks down. He is ashamed.)

BUELO: I sorry.

VICKY: It's okay. It's not like I expected you to testify against your own grandson. You afraid of him too, huh? Sometimes he's so nice, you know. So nice. And then other times, well, you saw. It's funny, you know, Rosario beat me so I left him for a cop and now the cop beats me. Oh yeah. Eight months pregnant and his aim is better than Rosario's. Who am I supposed to date next, the Pope? Tell you something, when the cop hits me it doesn't hurt as much as when Rosario did. Cause I don't love the cop. I'm stupid, huh? Have you seen his new girlfriend? I don't care, you know, we're over. I'm just curious is all.

(BUELO *offers her a cigarette.* ROSARIO *enters.*)

ROSARIO: You shouldn't be smoking.

(VICKY *takes the cigarette and lights it.*)

VICKY: Don't tell me what to do.

(ROSARIO *looks at her dark glasses.*)

ROSARIO: What happened to you?

VICKY: I ran into a door.

(*Silence*)

VICKY: (*Continuing*) Haven't seen you much.

ROSARIO: Well, that's what you wanted.

VICKY: Make no mistake about that.

ROSARIO: You should put some ice on that.

(ROSARIO *helps* BUELO *stand.*)

VICKY: Rosario.

ROSARIO: What?

VICKY: What's her name? Fuck it, I don't want to know. Listen, you're not gonna see the baby.

ROSARIO: You already said that.

VICKY: Okay, just as long as we understand each other.

ROSARIO: You will let me see him just once, right? When you bring him back from the hospital?

VICKY: …Just once. And that's it.

ROSARIO: I promise you. You won't ever see me again.

(VICKY *reaches into her grocery bag and hands him some Oreos.*)

VICKY: Here.

(ROSARIO *doesn't move.*)

ROSARIO: They belong to Officer J Clark.

(VICKY *forces them on him.*)

VICKY: He can just kiss my ass.

(ROSARIO *opens the pack and begins to eat one.*)

ROSARIO: Now I know why he hit you.

(ROSARIO *exits into the S R O with* BUELO.)

VICKY: He doesn't hit me! He doesn't! He loves me! (*She bangs on the door. Continuing*) You hear me? You got that? He loves me! He loves me! He loves me!

(ROSARIO *enters S R O room pushing a crib. It dominates the room.*)

BUELO: ¿Que's eso?

POPS: What the…?

ROSARIO: Top of the line. This is the best money can buy. I had to put it together in the hall. We got more space in the hall than we do in this damn room.

(ROSARIO *pushes it to the center of the room, forcing both* POPS *and* BUELO *to move.*)

POPS: Don't you think it looks ridiculous here?

ROSARIO: No, I think you look ridiculous here.

POPS: I still don't believe Vicky's gonna give you the baby.

ROSARIO: You don't have to believe it.

(He sees BUELO *playing with one of the built-in toys on the crib.)*

ROSARIO: *(Continuing)* Hey! Leave that alone.

*(*BUELO *sits.)*

POPS: He don't understand English.

ROSARIO: No, but he understands a tone of voice. *(Referring to the porno tape playing on the T V.)* And this has got to go.

*(*ROSARIO *turns it off.)*

BUELO: Hey.

ROSARIO: From now on only classy things. You want to watch that stuff go to some porno theatre.

*(*ROSARIO *turns on the radio, searches and finds a classical station.)*

BUELO: *¿Que dijo?*

POPS: *Callate viejo. (To* ROSARIO*)* I know you don't think we're gonna be listening to that all day.

ROSARIO: Successful people are successful because of the environment. It's a little sacrifice for my son. It's good music. Come on, don't you think it's good.

POPS: Okay. Why is it good?

ROSARIO: Cause.

POPS: No, why? You don't know shit about that music. I know about music. How do you know this is better?

*(*BUELO *leans back on the bed, covers his eyes and naps.)*

ROSARIO: Cause the people who like it are better.

POPS: Than who?

ROSARIO: Than us.

(POPS *goes to fridge, gets a beer and opens it.*)

POPS: Can we still drink beer? Or is that gonna screw up the kid that Vicky's never gonna give you.

ROSARIO: *(Under his breath.)* Fuck you.

(POPS *grabs* ROSARIO's *arm.*)

POPS: What did you say?

ROSARIO: I said Fuck You! I'm sorry if me wanting a better life for my son is such a crime. Maybe if you had done the same thing for me my life might be different.

POPS: Hey, that's not my [fault.]

ROSARIO: No, of course not. *(Silence)* Sons are supposed to move ahead, not be trapped. What did you ever want for me? *(Silence)* What did you [want for me?]

POPS: I wanted…you to take care of me. Like I'm taking care of my father.

ROSARIO: A servant.

(POPS *drains his beer.*)

POPS: You want one?

(ROSARIO *shakes his head.* POPS *puts his hand on* ROSARIO's *shoulder, who shakes it off.* ROSARIO *raises the volume on the music.* POPS *sits in front of the TV, he turns it on and porn sounds begin.* ROSARIO *moves the crib until he finds the ideal place for it.* ROSARIO *places a pillow in the center of the bed, he takes* BUELO's *cane and brings it over his head.*)

ROSARIO: *(Whispers)* Goodbye, Vicky. Whoosh!

(*Slaps are heard from behind* VICKY's *door. She hurries out and collapses outside the door, crying as the COP inside rages.*)

COP: *(V O)* Goddamn bitch! Still can't figure out where my socks are supposed to go. I tell her and tell her. *(He fades.)*

POPS: You think I'm a bad father? You think you gonna do better?

ROSARIO: Couldn't do worse.

(ROSARIO *exits.* POPS *picks up the pillow, holding it like a baby.)*

POPS: Before you were born I belonged to a little trio. Trios were very big back then, Los Diamantes, Los Condes, music like you don't hear anymore. Kiko worked in a bodega then and we would rehearse in the storeroom at night after he closed up shop. I was a tenor back then. You look surprised. I didn't always have this voice. I once had the voice of an angel. You could ask anybody, they'd all tell you, "That Ramon, he can really sing". We almost got a record contract. But, less than a year after Junior was born you came along. Your mother said I had to start working overtime, so I did. Around that time Kiko's wife left him, so he had that to deal with. It's like our dream just faded. Died a nice little natural death, you know. Hey, it happens.

(The sound of a toilet flushing off stage)

POPS: The third guy in the trio still sings. He joined another trio and they sing in Puerto Rico. He lives off it. How about that? He lives off his singing. It's funny. He had the worst voice of all of us. Not that it matters.

(Music: The Walk to the Paradise Garden *from* Romeo and Juliet *begins to play.* MORRIS *lights two cigarettes at once. He keeps one in his mouth and holds the other one out to an imaginary companion.)*

MORRIS: Oh, are you alone, too?

(Lights slowly up on window where ROSARIO *appears.)*

ACT TWO

ROSARIO: Hey.

(Lights up on DR MORTON's *office. He sits on his desk as* VICKY *stares off.)*

VICKY: I was a good girl.

DR MORTON: Fifteen thousand. A new life. Vicky?

ROSARIO: Psst.

MORRIS: *(To his imaginary companion)* You're a very beautiful boy. Tell me, you have no intention of dying anytime soon, do you?

ROSARIO: Psst, hey.

(MORRIS *drops both cigarettes and steps on them, putting them out.)*

POPS: I once had the voice of an angel.

DR MORTON: A new life.

ROSARIO: I need you. Make me over.

VICKY: I was a good girl before I took up with Rosario. You ask anybody and they'll tell you the same thing. "Vicky, she's a good girl". I wasn't allowed to date, couldn't have friends over. My father would point to my mother and say, "You want a better friend than your mother? That's your friend. That's the only friend you need."

DR MORTON: I'm sure it was very difficult for you.

VICKY: I was sixteen when I first saw Rosario.

DR MORTON: He's no longer your problem.

VICKY: Look, I can't sell my baby.

DR MORTON: It's fifteen thousand. All for you. To start a new life.

VICKY: ...In cash?

DR MORTON: Cashier's check.

VICKY: Cash!

DR MORTON: It's as good as cash.

VICKY: No, cash is as good as cash.

DR MORTON: You expect me to carry around fifteen thousand dollars in cash?

VICKY: Why not? Your customers expect me to carry a baby for them. You tell them I only speak cash. That's it.

DR MORTON: Vicky, you shouldn't think of them as customers.

VICKY: I hate being pregnant, you know? My skin doesn't fit. How did this happen? It used to fit. Just right. As if it were meant for me. It scares me. What if I stay like this, if I pop the baby and still look like a whale? His new girlfriend is probably thin. Thin and white.

DR MORTON: You're a very attractive young lady.

VICKY: Would you do me?

DR MORTON: I'm sorry. Excuse me?

VICKY: I don't mean right now, I mean… Nothing.

(Lights out on DR MORTON's office.)

MORRIS: Well, let's see. You think you're too good for where you are and you're not quite good enough for where you want to be. Quite a dilemma.

ROSARIO: I could…

MORRIS: You can nothing.

ROSARIO: But I want it so much.

MORRIS: Hunger is not the only criteria. So sorry. There's nothing in this for me, except aggravation.

ROSARIO: If not for me, do it for my son.

ACT TWO

MORRIS: This is a very bad time for me. I've come down with a terrible case of indifference.

ROSARIO: What do you want? I have another shirt.

MORRIS: I've had your shirt. ...If I thought you might be able to learn it might be worth my time.

ROSARIO: I can learn.

MORRIS: Very well then. A sock. But you must take if off on the window ledge.

(ROSARIO *places his hand on the glass,* MORRIS *echoes his movement, for a moment they seem to be touching through the glass.*)

ROSARIO: It would be easier if I were inside.

MORRIS: But I don't want it to be easier for you. I want my money's worth.

(MORRIS *turns away from* ROSARIO *who begins to untie his right shoe, take it off and very carefully remove the sock.*)

MORRIS: Do hurry with that sock.

ROSARIO: Why?

MORRIS: Unlike you I have things to do. A life to lead.

(ROSARIO *purposely drops the sock.*)

MORRIS: What have you done?!

ROSARIO: I dropped it. Since when did you want it so badly?

MORRIS: Since you dropped it.

ROSARIO: I got another one.

MORRIS: It's not the same thing.

ROSARIO: You're right. It's rarer. It's one of a kind.

(ROSARIO *removes his sock in the same manner as the other one. This time* MORRIS *watches intently, making sure no harm comes to the sock.*)

ROSARIO: Why do you want it so badly?

MORRIS: I don't.

ROSARIO: *(He feigns dropping the sock.)* Ooops.

MORRIS: All right, I do. I do. I want your heat. Your body heat. It's almost as if there were someone with me. Holding me.

ROSARIO: How much would you give me if I held you?

MORRIS: It's the facsimile I want! Not the real thing.

(ROSARIO *holds up the sock.*)

ROSARIO: Open the window.

(MORRIS *does. He takes the sock and holds it close.* ROSARIO *enters.*)

MORRIS: He's dead, you know. The beautiful boy is dead.

ROSARIO: What do you do with my clothes?

MORRIS: I wear them for a while, then I burn them.

ROSARIO: Must be nice to be rich.

MORRIS: Hey, I'm inside, you're trying to get in. You figure it out.

ROSARIO: Yeah, I guess one of us is trapped.

MORRIS: You never cease to amaze me, except of course when you don't.

ROSARIO: I want to start from scratch. Erase everything, all the mistakes. You know, I could never understand people when they say "I would do everything the same way." Hell no. You get a second chance and you would repeat every stupid thing all over again? Like the first time wasn't bad enough? You would change everything, wouldn't you?

(MORRIS *smacks the back of* ROSARIO's *head.*)

ACT TWO

MORRIS: The past does not exist. Rosario, if I'm going to make you over that is lesson one.

ROSARIO: You wouldn't even redo the bad things?

MORRIS: Given the proper spin nothing is wrong. Sin ceases to exist. Now smile. Erase the anger.

ROSARIO: The only legacy I have for my son is my anger. You can make me over, but leave that alone. Touch that and I'll kill you.

MORRIS: And that's why you'll never win. The second you show your anger the other person has won. Lesson two. You can be as angry as you want. Just never show it.

ROSARIO: How do you do that?

MORRIS: All right, off with you. Go find some beauty.

ROSARIO: Where?

(BUELO *stands outside of Junior's jail. He waves up to him. He shakes his head and begins to tap his cane.*)

BUELO: ¿A que le temo? A nada. A todo. A todo lo que esta fuera de mi control. Se controla, se es dueño de tan poco.

(ROSARIO *appears. He begins to drag* BUELO *away.*)

ROSARIO: Come on.

BUELO: ¿A donde vamos?

(*Slides of artwork flash on and off, over them, around them and right through them. The impression should be of* ROSARIO *trying to see as much art as possible in as little time as possible.*)

ROSARIO: Come on, try to act like you've been in a museum before.

(ROSARIO *drags* BUELO *who has a hard time keeping up.*)

ROSARIO: See how people look at this stuff, I mean this art. You step back, you don't want to be right on top of it and you nod while you're looking at it, like you're agreeing with the artist. And you turn to the person next to you and whisper something and they nod too. Nod your head.

BUELO: *¿Como fue?*

ROSARIO: *Nod. Di que si.*

BUELO: *Si.*

ROSARIO: No, with your head.

(ROSARIO *grabs* BUELO's *head and makes him nod.* ROSARIO *notices someone staring at them as he is teaching* BUELO *to nod.*)

ROSARIO: *(Pointing to painting)* We get it. ...We were just whispering how much we get it. *(He smiles at the person as they leave. Continuing)* I've got to learn all this. When I bring my son to museums and the theater and places like that he's not going to be ashamed of me. Cause I'm gonna get it. And I'm going to teach him how to get it, too. Okay, come on, we got ground to cover.

MORRIS: You're not doing the express check out lane for art. Let the work breathe.

ROSARIO: Yeah well, I don't have a lot of time. ... That's when I heard these people talking in Spanish. High brow people, not the guard, people with money. Spanish people with money, I knew they existed, I had just never seen them before. And I watched them, all dressed up, with their dressed up kids. Here was proof that it can be done.

MORRIS: Did they notice you?

ROSARIO: Of course not.

MORRIS: Of course not.

BUELO: *Cuatro, doce, diezinueve, vientiuno.*

ACT TWO 41

ROSARIO: Yeah, okay. Come on, Buelo, let's play your numbers. You say a person is born with their luck, I'm gonna make my son's luck.

(They return to the S R O where BUELO *collapses in his chair.* POPS *enters. Upon seeing him* ROSARIO *heads to the door.)*

POPS: Where you going?

ROSARIO: Out.

POPS: You're not gonna cook?

ROSARIO: You'll manage.

POPS: Vicky came by today.

ROSARIO: What?!

POPS: She asked about the crib.

*(*ROSARIO *bolts out.* POPS *calls out after him.)*

BUELO: *Cuatro, doce, diezinueve, vientiuno.*

POPS: Hey, don't forget to play Buelo's numbers!

*(*VICKY *at* DR MORTON's *office.* ROSARIO *arrives outside the office and overhears the end of their conversation.)*

DR MORTON: ...Vicky, they might go as high as twenty. Cash. You have to think of what's best for the baby. And for you.

VICKY: Rosario brought the baby a crib. He wanted to surprise me with it.

*(*ROSARIO *enters.)*

ROSARIO: Sorry I'm late.

DR MORTON: We don't have an appointment today.

ROSARIO: Gee Vicky, you come here more than I do. You sleeping with the good doctor?

VICKY: See, this is why we can't have a conversation. *(She takes her bag and exits.)*

ROSARIO: What's she doing here?

DR MORTON: Maybe she's more interested in bettering herself than you are.

ROSARIO: Yeah, there's always that.

DR MORTON: I have a lot of work, Rosario. So why don't you come back when you do have an appointment.

ROSARIO: How much do you make a year?

DR MORTON: I don't think that's any of your business.

ROSARIO: Just curious. I hope they pay you well. You being an expert and all. You giving Vicky good advice?

DR MORTON: I'm not at liberty to say.

ROSARIO: She's a whore, you know. I'm just saying. I mean, she's pregnant and she's working in this bar. Is that in your report?

DR MORTON: You beat your girlfriend, you kicked her—

ROSARIO: Does one mistake take away everything else about me?

DR MORTON: Did you beat her once?

ROSARIO: Hey, were you there? Did you see what she did to me?

DR MORTON: What did she do to you?

ROSARIO: …She made me mad.

DR MORTON: So you almost killed her because she made you mad? Did you ever make her mad? Am I making you mad right now, Rosario? Of course if you touched me I would make sure that you would never see daylight again. Like your brother. *(Silence)* Did she make you madder than I just did? Try not to be late for your next appointment. *(Silence)* That's all, Rosario. You can go now. I'm dismissing you.

ACT TWO 43

ROSARIO: You ever get any real crazies? Not like me, but somebody who just doesn't give a shit.

DR MORTON: I've never met anybody who didn't care what happened to them. I find that most bullies are cowards.

ROSARIO: Yeah, they are. They hide behind a desk—

DR MORTON: Or a fist.

ROSARIO: Yeah, well you know better. You're the expert. Whatever they're paying you, it's not enough. …What's that music?

DR MORTON: There is no—

ROSARIO: Mozart. *Concerto for Flute and String in F Major*.

DR MORTON: There is no music.

ROSARIO: Of course not. Who said there was? Gotta go. I'm taking Buelo to the museum.

DR MORTON: The museum?

ROSARIO: Oh yeah. We just started going. Somebody I know tells me which one to go to and what to look at. I'm gonna get smart enough to have a conversation with you, huh Doctor.

(Sounds of breaking dishes and furniture. Lights out on DR MORTON's office as ROSARIO exits. Lights come up to dim outside of VICKY's door. She steps outside her door as COP continues on his rampage.)

COP: *(V O)* Goddamn it, you think I'm fucking kidding you?! You think I'm playing with you, bitch?!

VICKY: I'll call your wife on you, I will. Don't think I won't. *(To herself)* Bastard. *(She touches the spot on her face where she was struck. Continuing)* Jesus. *(She pulls out her cigarettes, she takes one and retrieves her lighter from her bag.)*

(When VICKY *lights her cigarette* ROSARIO *lights his off to the side. He watches her as she puts back the lighter. When she does she pulls out the silver spoon he had given her. She stares at it.)*

ROSARIO: *(Sings softly)* Hey everybody have you heard.

VICKY: What do you want?

ROSARIO: Nothing.

VICKY: That'll be the day.

ROSARIO: What's he doing in there? Redecorating?

VICKY: Making room for the new baby stuff. *(To inside door)* Yeah, baby, you just get rid of whatever we don't need.

ROSARIO: Sounds like he's drunk.

VICKY: Why? Is that what your father sounds like?

(Silence. The noise from inside stops. A frightened VICKY *looks at the door.)*

ROSARIO: Relax. He's out for the night.

VICKY: It's not like that.

ROSARIO: Trust me. *(He takes the cigarette out of her mouth and puts it out.)* You shouldn't—

*(*VICKY *takes the cigarette out of* ROSARIO's *mouth and smokes it.)*

ROSARIO: —smoke.

VICKY: I saw the crib. Thank you. You didn't have to do that.

ROSARIO: Why? Your boyfriend already got him one?

VICKY: As a matter of fact, yes he did.

ROSARIO: Not better than mine. Mine is top of the line.

VICKY: I'm surprised your new girlfriend let you spend the money.

ACT TWO 45

ROSARIO: She knows how to shut up and listen.

VICKY: Oh, so she's a bigger fool than I was?

ROSARIO: Nobody's that big a fool.

(ROSARIO *and* VICKY *laugh, relax a bit.*)

VICKY: She treat you nice?

(ROSARIO *nods.*)

ROSARIO: She treats me with respect.

VICKY: Do you remember why you hit me?

(ROSARIO *takes his cigarette back.*)

ROSARIO: I'll see you at the doctor's. (*He begins to leave.*)

VICKY: Cause you were mad at your father. Make sure she's not around when your father gets you pissed off.

(BUELO *sits on the bed in the S R O. He taps his cane repeatedly on the floor as he rocks himself back and forth.* POPS *stands over him trying to comfort him.*)

BUELO: *Seguro que no, seguro que no, seguro que no.*

(ROSARIO *leaves* VICKY *and enters S R O. Lights out on* VICKY)

ROSARIO: What's with Buelo?

POPS: Where were you?

ROSARIO: I was out. Thinking.

POPS: All night?

ROSARIO: What? Is there a time limit?

POPS: His numbers came out.

ROSARIO: What?

POPS: All of them. Four, twelve, nineteen, twenty one. Like God himself picked them out of a barrel.

ROSARIO: Today?

POPS: You were supposed to play his numbers.

ROSARIO: I forgot.

POPS: They told me you never showed up.

(ROSARIO *kneels by* BUELO.)

ROSARIO: I'm sorry, Buelo.

POPS: Quarter of a million.

(BUELO *kisses* ROSARIO'*s head*.)

ROSARIO: I was thinking about my baby, you know… I'm sorry, Buelo.

BUELO: *Dile que no tengo coraje.*

POPS: He said he's not mad.

ROSARIO: Of course he is. *Si*, Buelo, you're very mad.

(BUELO *shakes his head "no"*.)

ROSARIO: You waited all your life for your one piece of luck.

BUELO: *Cada persona nace con su suerte.*

POPS: Everybody is born with their luck.

BUELO: *Mi suerte fue perder.*

POPS: My luck was to lose.

ROSARIO: That's not true.

BUELO: *Somos perdedores*, Rosario.

POPS: We are losers.

ROSARIO: Tell him not to say that.

BUELO: *Dios me castigo por desear demasiado.*

POPS: God punished me for wanting too much.

(ROSARIO *grabs the cane from* BUELO, *stopping the incessant tapping*.)

ROSARIO: No! God did not place us on this earth to lose.

BUELO: *Uno se tiene que reconocer.*

ACT TWO

POPS: You gotta accept what you are.

BUELO: *Yo, tu padre, tu y tu hijo.*

POPS: Me, your father, you and your son.

(ROSARIO *raises the cane to strike* BUELO. POPS *pushes* ROSARIO *and grabs* BUELO, *pulling him up from the bed.* ROSARIO *regains his balance and brings the cane crashing down where* BUELO *sat.*)

ROSARIO: My son is not gonna be like us. He is not gonna be anything like us.

BUELO: *¿Y como va ser?!*

(Silence)

ROSARIO: What did he say?

POPS: Nothing. Come on, Rosario, [calm down.]

ROSARIO: What did he say?!

POPS: He asked…what would your son be like.

(ROSARIO *looks at himself and throws the cane on the bed.*)

ROSARIO: …Not like us.

BUELO: *Uno nace con su suerte.*

POPS: You're born with your luck.

ROSARIO: I'm gonna make sure the kind of luck he's born with.

(VICKY *enters* DR MORTON's *office.* ROSARIO *enters and sits by her, he notices she is wearing dark glasses.*)

VICKY: Don't say anything.

(DR MORTON *enters.*)

DR MORTON: Is there any reason you're wearing dark glasses indoors, Vicky?

VICKY: No.

DR MORTON: Why don't you take them off.

(VICKY *hesitates, then takes off her sunglasses to reveal a black eye.*)

ROSARIO: *(Under his breath)* I knew it.

VICKY: Shut up.

DR MORTON: Rosario…I'm speechless. How could you do this?

ROSARIO: Hey, I didn't touch her.

VICKY: He didn't.

DR MORTON: Please don't cover up for him. It helps no one.

ROSARIO: That did not come from me.

DR MORTON: Where then?

VICKY: I ran into a door.

DR MORTON: Please Vicky. Where did it come from, Rosario?

ROSARIO: I think the lady answered you.

DR MORTON: I want you to answer me.

VICKY: He didn't do it!

ROSARIO: My answer is I didn't do it. Followed by my question, "How come you get to call us by our first name and we still gotta call you Doctor?"

DR MORTON: Don't try to change the subject.

ROSARIO: No Morton, Mort, Mo, why is that? I seem to be in a bit of a quandary over that.

(*Bach's* Concerto in G Minor *begins to play softly in the background.* VICKY *and* DR MORTON *stare at* ROSARIO *in shock.*)

ROSARIO: Why it seems to me that the good doctor is at a loss for words. How very unlike you. Don't tell me you've used up all the ones you know. That would be a tragedy, wouldn't it.

ACT TWO

DR MORTON: I think…sit down.

ROSARIO: Oh good, you still know four. That's a comfort. I didn't mean to tax you. Perhaps a beverage would bring the color back to your cheeks. Martini?

DR MORTON: I am going to have to write you up.

ROSARIO: I hope you also write how you called this lady a liar. If she says nothing happened then it is your duty to believe her. A gentleman would do no less. Come Victoria, we will leave the good doctor to his endless paperwork and the pounding migraine that seems to have overcome him.

(ROSARIO *extends his arm to* VICKY *who takes it in a daze.* DR MORTON *rises.*)

DR MORTON: Vick—Ms Suarez, I…

ROSARIO: As always doctor, you've been the perfect host. Hey Mort, I'll give you five hundred dollars for your pants!

DR MORTON: What?!

ROSARIO: Uh, goodbye, I mean.

(*Escorting* VICKY *out.*)

ROSARIO: I was doing so well, too. You got an aspirin?

(*Lights out on* DR MORTON*'s office.*)

VICKY: Who was that?

ROSARIO: The new Rosario.

VICKY: …You want to walk me home?

ROSARIO: So when are you due?

VICKY: Any day now.

ROSARIO: You'll let me see him, won't you? Before you take him away forever. At your place with just you. Can you do that for me?

VICKY: Okay.

(ROSARIO *starts off.*)

VICKY: Rosario.

ROSARIO: What?

VICKY: Nothing. I just wanted to look at you, that's all.

(VICKY *disappears into her area as* ROSARIO *enters* MORRIS's *area.*)

MORRIS: So you sounded just like me. How very sweet. My mother had a pet monkey she taught to drink brandy out of a snifter.

ROSARIO: I'm not a monkey.

MORRIS: Who said you were? This monkey amused all our guests. And, it knew it's place.

ROSARIO: What would happen to you if I hung you outside by your heels?

MORRIS: The headline would read, "Extraordinary White Man Dies". What do you think yours would read?

(ROSARIO *grabs* MORRIS *by the neck.*)

MORRIS: Who was Mendelssohn? (*Pause*) Your son will have to know, even if you don't.

ROSARIO: You don't fight fair.

MORRIS: I don't have to.

ROSARIO: Does that mean I don't have to either?

MORRIS: Lesson three.

(*Lights fade on them as the sounds of a baby being delivered are heard.* ROSARIO *is seen holding the cane, poised as if to strike.*)

ROSARIO: Goodbye Vicky. Whoosh!

(ROSARIO *enters carrying* BUELO's *cane.* VICKY *stands outside her door. She is no longer pregnant.* ROSARIO *stands at least six feet away from her.*)

ACT TWO   51

VICKY: Hi.

ROSARIO: Hi.

VICKY: Am I going to have to yell so you can hear me?

ROSARIO: What about Officer Clark?

VICKY: He's on duty.

(ROSARIO *comes closer.*)

VICKY: Did you hurt yourself?

ROSARIO: No. Why?

VICKY: The cane.

ROSARIO: I thought you could use it. After giving birth and all.

(VICKY *moves closer to* ROSARIO *and tries to take his hand. He pulls away.*)

VICKY: When I first saw you I flipped. I thought you were the cutest boy in the world. I remember the teacher yelled at you for something and a week later you tripped him.

ROSARIO: I did not.

VICKY: I saw it. Mister Sisko went flying with all of his test papers.

(ROSARIO *smiles.*)

VICKY: You made that same smile.

(ROSARIO *turns from her, he grabs the cane with both hands and braces himself to kill her.* VICKY *speaks to his back.*)

VICKY: Maybe that's when I fell in love with you. I love you, I always have. ...I want us to try again. Don't say no, please. Please.

(ROSARIO *turns to face* VICKY. *She gently holds his face.*)

VICKY: You are so totally wrong for me. (*She kisses his face. Continuing*) I have a confession to make to you. I was gonna sell our baby. I know, I know, it was wrong and I thought I could, but I can't. Cause it's ours. And I want us to raise it. Together.

(ROSARIO *drops the cane and kisses* VICKY.)

VICKY: I'll move my things back in with you.

ROSARIO: Okay.

VICKY: And maybe we can get a place of our own?

ROSARIO: Yeah, sure. I'm gonna be getting some money soon. Don't worry. I'll take care of everything. I love you.

VICKY: Come on in, take a look at your son.

(ROSARIO *follows her inside.*)

(*Lights out as* ROSARIO *exits. The light from the T V screen in the S R O comes up illuminating the room. Pops sits in his chair watching a porno tape. The sound of the porno tape is all we hear at first, until* BUELO, *who is sitting next to* POPS *opens his beer. The sound of the porno tape slowly fade as we hear* ROSARIO *singing softly as he enters carrying his baby.*)

ROSARIO: Hey everybody have you heard, I'm gonna buy him a mocking bird... (*He continues softly.*)

(ROSARIO *heads to* DR MORTON's *office.* VICKY *enters the S R O. She carries her belongings in some cheap nylon gym bags. Neither* POPS *or* BUELO *see her enter.*)

ROSARIO & VICKY: Surprise.

(ROSARIO *sees there is no one in the doctor's office. He sits and waits. In the S R O,* VICKY *clears her throat,* POPS *continues watching his movie; only* BUELO *acknowledges her.*)

ROSARIO: (*Speaking to his son*) Your mother saved her life today.

BUELO: *Mi'ja.*

ACT TWO 53

VICKY: I'm back. *(Silence)* Rosario told you I was coming back, right?

POPS: Yeah, but I didn't think you were stupid enough to actually do it.

VICKY: I could use some help with my things.

(BUELO *tries to stand to help* VICKY *with her things.*)

POPS: *(To* BUELO*)* Where you going? You lost your cane, sit the hell down.

(BUELO *sits back down.* VICKY *looks around and puts her belongings down.*)

VICKY: We'll get you another cane, Buelo. Gold tipped.

POPS: Yeah, right.

VICKY: Some things never change. Is that the same tape you had when I left here? Is it on a goddamn loop?

POPS: No. Rosario brought me a bunch of new tapes, okay? For me, for me and Buelo.

VICKY: You're not gonna watch that crap when my son is here. *(Silence)* You're not. Cause we're starting a new life, you know.

ROSARIO: New life.

VICKY: And us being here with you all is only temporary. We're gonna get out own apartment—

POPS: Yeah, right.

VICKY: —and everything. You watch.

ROSARIO: New life.

VICKY: Cause he loves me and he loves our son. And I can't believe you would watch those tapes when your grandson is here.

POPS: But he's not here, is he?

VICKY: I mean when he's here.

POPS: But he's not here, is he?

VICKY: But he will be. Soon.

ROSARIO: New life.

(VICKY *looks around the room.* BUELO *hands her his beer.*)

BUELO: *Mi'ja.*

(VICKY *opens her beer, not finding anyplace to sit, she gets into the crib. She pulls her legs up close to her.*)

POPS: Look at the tits on that one.

(*Lights dim on S R O as* DR MORTON *enters his office.*)

ROSARIO: Surprise.

DR MORTON: What are you doing here?

ROSARIO: Expecting Vicky? Expecting Vicky and my son? Have you met him?

DR MORTON: No.

ROSARIO: Trevor, this is Doctor Morton, the man who wanted to sell you.

DR MORTON: Trevor Cortez?

ROSARIO: Well, I'll have to change my name because it won't go with his. I believe you have some money for my son. Not for my son, in exchange for my son.

DR MORTON: Vicky—

ROSARIO: Told me all about it. Twenty thousand, right? What do you think, is he worth it? Do we look alike?

DR MORTON: You would sell him?

ROSARIO: You would buy him?

DR MORTON: A couple I know would. A healthy male baby.

ROSARIO: And that twenty thousand dollars could give Vicky a new life. So, you got the money?

(ROSARIO *pulls* BUELO's *cane from the back of his belt.*)

ACT TWO

DR MORTON: You don't want to do this, Rosario.

ROSARIO: Neither do you, that's why you asked Vicky to meet you after everybody had gone. So you got the money?

DR MORTON: No.

ROSARIO: And it's in cash, right? I know Vicky, she's a cash up front kind of gal.

(ROSARIO *lifts the cane.* DR MORTON *goes for his phone,* ROSARIO *sweeps it off his desk with the cane.*)

ROSARIO: The money, Doctor. New lives don't come cheap. Old ones do, though.

DR MORTON: I'm going to give you the money and then you're going to leave. And neither one of us will ever mention it. I will forget I ever saw you.

ROSARIO: My son and I are leaving. To start a new adventure. You'll wish us well?

DR MORTON: I'll wish you well.

ROSARIO: That means so much to me.

(ROSARIO *brings the cane crashing down on* DR MORTON's *leg.* DR MORTON *crumples, he raises his hands to protect himself.*)

DR MORTON: Please.

ROSARIO: The money.

(DR MORTON *pulls an envelope out of his coat pocket.*)

DR MORTON: You don't want your son to be ashamed of you, do you Rosario? *(Silence)* Take the money, and you can both go. And I'll never tell.

ROSARIO: Nope. You never will.

(*Lights out on* VICKY *and* DR MORTON's *office. Lights up on* MORRIS *who stands looking out his window. Chopin's* Fantasie Impromptu *is heard.*)

MORRIS: Streaks. Why is it so hard to get good help nowadays? What is your son going to be when he grows up?

(ROSARIO *enters carrying his baby,* MORRIS's *back is to them.*)

ROSARIO: White.

MORRIS: What is your son going to be when he grows up?

ROSARIO: Right.

MORRIS: I heard you the first time.

ROSARIO: I came to say good-bye.

MORRIS: You're leaving?

ROSARIO: I got my one piece of luck today. My son and I are off to start a new life.

MORRIS: Speaking of the little anglophile, where is your son?

ROSARIO: Right here.

(MORRIS *turns to face them.*)

ROSARIO: Today we come in through the front door.

MORRIS: Oh, but the window suits you so.

ROSARIO: I killed someone today. And I wanted to kill my son's mother. The only reason I didn't [was because...]

(MORRIS *smacks the back of* ROSARIO's *head, just as* POPS *and* BUELO *did.*)

MORRIS: The past does not exist.

ROSARIO: I need something from you. Your name. You're not using it, you pathetic, lonely old man.

MORRIS: I'm not that old. What will you give me for it?

ACT TWO

(ROSARIO *takes out the blood soaked cane that has been hanging from the back of his belt.*)

MORRIS: Where will you go?

ROSARIO: Somewhere there's an even playing field for my son.

MORRIS: I designed the playing field, I approve all the changes. It'll never be even.

ROSARIO: Someday, you know, he'll wear a tie to work and people like you will have to call him "sir." You think he'll forgive me, right?

MORRIS: He has nothing to forgive you for. You went out and got what you needed. By any means possible. He will be very proud of you.

(ROSARIO *hands* MORRIS *the cane.*)

MORRIS: Morris. The name is Morris.

ROSARIO: Who will you be if I take your name?

(MORRIS *shrugs and turns up the music. He turns away and begins to conduct his imaginary orchestra.* ROSARIO *gently touches his back,* MORRIS *violently shakes him off. He raises the cane.*)

MORRIS: No! No touching! You are never to touch me.

ROSARIO: You know, I almost always kind of liked you. Bless him.

(MORRIS *and* ROSARIO *stare at each other.* MORRIS *lowers the cane down to his side.*)

MORRIS: All hail the beautiful boy.

(ROSARIO *and son exit.*)

MORRIS: Where will you go?

(*Lights up on S R O.* VICKY *sits in the crib as* BUELO *strokes her hair.*)

VICKY: He should be here any minute. With our son.

POPS: You planning on cooking tonight?

VICKY: He'll walk in through that door. Won't he? I was a good girl. When I first met Rosario.

(VICKY *raises the side of the crib, waiting inside the crib for* ROSARIO *who will never return.* ROSARIO *carries his son past the S R O, and heads off to a new life with his son.*)

ROSARIO: Hey everybody have you heard
I'm gonna buy him a mockingbird
And if that mockingbird don't sing
I'm gonna buy him—everything.
(Spoken) Everything for you, Mister Trevor Morris.

(*Lights fade on* MORRIS *and S R O as* ROSARIO *carries his son off stage.*)

END OF PLAY

www.ingramcontent.com/pod-product-compliance
Lightning Source LLC
Chambersburg PA
CBHW060219050426
42446CB00013B/3108